DRAMA•DANCE•SINGING

TEACHER RESOURCE BOOK

Edited by
John Nicholas

Dramatic Lines*

Drama • Dance • Singing
Teacher Resource Book
text copyright © Stagecoach Theatre Arts Regional Schools Ltd

A CIP record for this book is available from the British Library

ISBN 0 9537770 2 2

Drama • Dance • Singing
Teacher Resource Book
first published in 2001
by
Dramatic Lines
Twickenham England
All rights reserved

Printed by The Dramatic Lines Press
Twickenham England

FOREWORD

I was pleased to be asked to write a foreword for this innovative and unusual book inspired by Stagecoach Theatre Arts and containing contributions by its teaching staff.

In these days it is so important for young people to have opportunities to discover their abilities and talents and find their self esteem. It is equally important that they learn to communicate with others creatively and confidently. These opportunities are now widely offered by organisations who teach performing skills in small classes. The value to young people of such activities is incalculable

For those professionals who work with young people in dance, drama and singing, this book is a valuable resource and I highly recommend it.

Phillip Schofield

This book
is
dedicated to the teachers of the
Stagecoach Theatre Arts Schools
who have contributed these
drama dance and singing
activities.

The stages indicated are a guide based on teachers personal use and almost all material has great flexibility without adaptation:

LEVEL GUIDE

EARLY STAGES •	under 7
STAGE 1 •	7 - 9
STAGE 2 •	10 - 12
STAGE 3 •	13 - 16

CONTENTS

DRAMA

DANCE

SINGING

DRAMA
SECTION

THE BAKER'S SHOP

"Who stole the bread from the Baker's shop?"
Employ a suitable rhythm, clapping or snapping fingers.

TEACHER: Who stole the bread from the Baker's shop?
Edward stole the bread from the Baker's shop.

EDWARD: Who me?

TEACHER: Yes, you!

EDWARD: Couldn't have been.

TEACHER: Well, who?

The rhythm continues with Edward taking control.

EDWARD: Sally stole the bread from the Baker's shop.

SALLY: Who me?

EDWARD: Yes, you!

SALLY: Couldn't have been.

EDWARD: Well, who?

SALLY: Louise stole the bread from the Baker's shop.

And on to the next child ....

- This is a wonderful way to learn each others names at the start of a new year.

Claire-Louise Dunteavy

DEAD LIONS

On the shout **"Dead Lions!"** all pupils drop to the floor. Absolutely no movement is allowed.

The teacher then tries to make individual lions move or laugh by 'intimidating' each of them in turn.

> *e.g.* "I'm going to tickle you."
> "A spider is about to crawl on your face."
> "Are you laughing?"
> "Did I see you blink?"
> *etc.*

N.B. No touching is permitted.

- Suitable for Early Stages students when needing to attract attention if matters are getting somewhat out of hand!

Jenny Billington

PRINCESS ZARA'S JEWELS

RESOURCES: • a treasure box full of plastic jewellery •
• a letter from Princess Zara •

PREPARATION: Hide the treasure box in the area that the children will be working.

MAIN ACTIVITY: Begin the lesson by showing the class Princess Zara's letter asking for their help in finding and returning her jewels that have been snatched by a wicked goblin.

The children search for the treasure and when it has been found discuss what to do next and how to get the jewels back to the princess and then write her a letter.

The children receive a present from Princess Zara the following week with a letter thanking them for their help.

N.B. The students find this powerful and engrossing because the teacher enters the world of the piece with them and becomes part of the drama. This technique also reaps rewards with the older groups, too.

- I have found that each Early Stages class acts very differently when the treasure is found. Some children are too busy trying on the jewellery to want to give it back, others offer to give Princess Zara some of their own and on one occasion a child sat on the box for the entire lesson in case the goblin crept up and snatched the treasure back again!

Trudy Hindmarsh

IN A DARK DARK WOOD

Younger children really enjoy acting out journeys.

The following poem can either be learnt or repeated line by line after the teacher, accompanied by appropriate actions:

In a dark, dark wood there was a dark, dark gate,
And through the dark, dark gate there was a dark, dark path,
And up the dark, dark path there was a dark, dark house,
And in the dark, dark house there was a dark, dark door,
And through the dark, dark door there was a dark, dark hall,
And in the dark, dark hall there was a dark, dark stair,
And up the dark, dark stair there was a dark, dark room,
And in the dark, dark room there was a dark, dark cupboard,
And in the dark, dark cupboard there was a dark, dark box,
And in the dark, dark box there was a ...... **GHOST!**

The children can add their own sound effects to the actions and come up with their own ideas as to what their surroundings are like.

e.g. deep mud beneath their feet in the wood
a bitterly cold windy night
a thunderstorm
a creaking gate and a hooting owl
a winding creaky staircase
a hall full of cobwebs
etc.

N.B. This poem is widely known and you will probably find that some of your pupils know a version of it. The exercise can last as long as you wish but I usually spend around fifteen minutes, and I always find that the children ask to do it again and again in later sessions.

• Build up the suspense towards the end and the children will adore being frightened by the ghost, even though they usually know what is coming.

Bethan Morgan

HALLOWEEN

WARM-UP: Sit in a circle. Discuss Halloween.

MAIN ACTIVITY: The teacher reads *Witches Spell:*

> Double, double, toil and trouble;
> Fire burn; and, cauldron bubble.
> Fillet of a fenny snake,
> In the cauldron boil and bake;
> Eye of newt, and toe of frog,
> Wool of bat, and tongue of dog,
> Adder's fork, and blind-worm's sting,
> Lizard's leg and owlet's wing, -
> For a charm of powerful trouble,
> Like a hell-broth, boil and bubble.
> Double, double, toil and trouble;
> Fire, burn, and, cauldron bubble.

> William Shakespeare

Ask the children to think up their own 'horrible' ingredients for a spell. Go round the circle. Each child in turn recites the first two lines of the poem, plus whatever is to be added to the pot.

> *e.g.* Double, double, toil and trouble;
> Fire burn; and, cauldron bubble.
> **A huge dinosaur egg!**
> In the cauldron boil and bake.

The child mimes putting this into the 'pot' in the centre of the circle thinking carefully about the size, weight, feel, smell, *etc.* Then the entire group repeats the lines and mime.

And so on round the circle ....

- Of course the children use the scariest, most horrible voices when speaking lines and pull faces into gruesome grimaces and grins!

ADDITIONAL RESOURCE: • Halloween • *Drama Lessons in Action*
Antoinette Line   ISBN 0 9522224 2 6   Dramatic Lines

Josephine Wells

STAGECRAFT GAME

This game teaches students the correct names for the different parts of the stage. Start by showing these areas and telling them the names.

> apron
> auditorium
> backcloth
> centre stage
> cyclorama
> downstage centre
> downstage left
> downstage right
> opposite prompt
> orchestra pit
> proscenium arch
> prompt corner
> stage left
> stage left wings
> stage right
> stage right wings
> upstage centre
> upstage left
> upstage right

Once the students have been shown turn it into a game. Call out the name for one of the positions. Instruct the children to run to this nominated area.

The game can be developed by adding actions for the different members of a company.

> *e.g.* actor
> musical director
> choreographer
> scene crew
> wig master
> lighting designer
> wardrobe mistress
> dresser
> *etc.*

- This can also work well as an elimination game.

BACKCLOTH OR CYCLORAMA		
UPSTAGE RIGHT	UPSTAGE CENTRE	UPSTAGE LEFT
STAGE RIGHT	CENTRE STAGE	STAGE LEFT
DOWNSTAGE RIGHT	DOWNSTAGE CENTRE	DOWNSTAGE LEFT

STAGE RIGHT WINGS

OPPOSITE PROMPT

STAGE LEFT WINGS

PROMPT CORNER

PROSCENIUM ARCH

APRON

ORCHESTRA PIT

AUDITORIUM

NON ACTING MEMBERS OF THE THEATRE COMPANY

BACK STAGE

ANGEL	financial backer.
PRODUCER	overall boss who arranges the show, employs the creative staff and pays the bills.
DIRECTOR	directs the actors, has overall control of the show.
CHOREOGRAPHER	designs dances and trains dancers.
MUSICAL DIRECTOR	directs singers and the orchestra.
DESIGNER	is in overall charge of the design of the show.
LIGHTING DESIGNER	designs lighting.
SOUND ENGINEER	is in charge of all sound.
STAGE MANAGER	organises everything backstage.
DEPUTY STAGE MANAGER	runs the show from prompt corner 'calls the show'
ASSISTANT STAGE MANAGER	looks after properties, 'props', makes tea, *etc.*
SCENE CREW	moves scenery.
FLYMAN	is in charge of scenery that is flown in from above.
WARDROBE MISTRESS	looks after the costumes.
WIG MASTER	looks after the wigs.
DRESSER	helps the actors into their clothes.
LX	deals with technical matters to do with sound, especially radio microphones, 'mikes'.
COMPANY MANAGER	looks after the actors wants and needs.

FRONT OF HOUSE

FRONT OF HOUSE MANAGER	in charge of programme sellers, ice cream vendors and stewards who take tickets, show people to their seats.
BOX OFFICE	sells the tickets.

Natalie Jones

ACTION DECISION GAME

Shout out the name of an area of the stage for the students to travel to, (See list on Page 6) and whilst they are on the move give them an action to perform, give an intention to do something that requires a response from them or tell them something that they must respond to in a prearranged way.

> *e.g.* "Sweep the stage." .. All mime the activity.
> "Flying overhead." .. All duck.
> *"Macbeth"* .... All turn to face downstage and "Shh".
> *etc.*

If students make a mistake or are slow to make a directional decision they are 'out' and retire to sit in the 'auditorium' as members of the audience. To increase the level of difficulty the audience (the players reference point) can be moved.

John Almond

THE WIZARD GAME

PREPARATION: Create an area that will represent the ramparts of the wizard's castle by placing five or six chairs a suitable distance from the wall at one end of the room.

MAIN ACTIVITY: Half the members of the class 'create' a wild forest that holds the wizard's secret treasure by pretending to be trees and bushes while the other half are explorers looking for treasure in the magic forest. The explorers must be careful not to touch the 'poisonous' trees and bushes.

The teacher is the wizard who imagines hearing or seeing some activity in the forest and comes out onto the castle ramparts to investigate. The Wizard then pops in and out frequently and the explorers must freeze or pretend to be trees to avoid being spotted.

The wizard finally enters the forest, the explorers leave immediately and the groups then change places.

Giuliano Neri

THE PIED PIPER OF HAMLIN

LESSON 1

• RECOUNT THE STORY

Sit in a circle and recount the story of *The Pied Piper* as a group.

• DISCUSS MEDIEVAL TIMES

"What did Hamlin look like in medieval times?"
Ask each child to name one thing that ***would not*** have been there in those days.

> *e.g.* electricity
> television
> cars
> *etc.*

Ask each child to name one thing that ***would*** have been seen there in those days.

> *e.g.* candles
> musical instruments
> horses
> *etc.*

• IN PAIRS

Explain that they are going to be the townspeople of Hamlin. Pairs talk and each person decides who they want to be.

> *i.e.* "What job do you do?"
> "What family do you have?"
> "How old are you?"
> *etc.*

N.B. Children cannot be younger than their actual age but may be of any age up to sixty. They must keep their own names (as it would be confusing to change).

In five minutes ask everyone to form a circle and each pair to introduce their partner.

> *e.g.* Lee is a cobbler aged thirty and has a daughter of six.
> Louise is a young widow, she works in the dairy making cheeses
> and has a son aged nine and daughter of seven.
> Sam is a child of eleven and has a younger brother and older sister.

Ask questions to fill out the character or correct information if necessary.

- SPONTANEOUS IMPROVISATION

The market place on market day. Pairs split and move to opposite sides of the room. On the count of three each child takes on the role of his/her character buying and selling in the market. The partners meet up and each tells the other about a rat that was sighted last night. Ask them to talk about it in detail.

> *i.e.* "Where was the rat?"
> "What did it look like?"
> "What did you do?"
> *etc.*

The townspeople then mingle and swap stories about the sighting of rats.

- TOWNSPEOPLE STILL IMAGE

Explain that all the townspeople are to freeze and capture the moment in a still picture when you clap three times. Shoulder tap volunteers to tell their personal rat story to the group.

- TOWN COUNCIL STILL IMAGE

Place a semicircle of chairs at one end of the room. Children in pairs decide which one is to be the Hamlin town councillor. Each town person leads the elected councillor to a chair in the council chamber and moulds this character into a still position portraying arrogance, snobbishness, snootiness, *etc.* Townspeople stand back and look at the still image of the town council they have created and make any necessary final adjustments to improve the picture.

LESSON 2

RESOURCES: • *large sheet of paper/card* • *felt tip pens* • *(TOWN PLAN)*
• *letter* • *scroll* • *sheets of A4 paper* • *pens/pencils* • *(LETTERS)*
• *2 sticks* • *(COUNCIL MEETING)*

WARM-UP: Talk about lesson 1 and make sure people remember who is who!

- TOWN PLAN

Ask each child or family group to draw their house and place of work. Create a map/town plan of Hamlin marking the river, town hall, council chamber and market square.

- TOWN COUNCIL STILL IMAGE

Recreate Lesson 1 still image of the town council. Explain that the meeting is about complaints concerning the rats received by Hamlin town council. None of the councillors believe the townspeople because they all live up on the hill in big houses and have not seen a single rat. Shoulder tap each councillor in turn to find out what they are saying or thinking at this meeting.

- TOWNSPEOPLE STILL IMAGE

The townspeople are growing more and more desperate because their complaints have been ignored by the councillors. They adopt a still image pose. Shoulder tap each person to find out what they are saying or thinking about this.

- LETTERS

N.B. Non-readers will need help.

Separate the two groups at opposite ends of the room. Give the councillors the letter to read and the scroll to the town crier to read aloud to the townspeople.

LETTER TO THE TOWN COUNCIL

Dear Hamlin Town Council

It has come to my attention that the lowly townsfolk of Hamlin have been spreading silly rumours about a plague of rats in our town. We, who live high up on the hillside, know this to be simply idle gossip, lies and superstition. I am sure you all agree that there are no rats in Hamlin. Please write to each person in the town telling them not to be unreasonable and to get back to work immediately.

Yours sincerely

I. M. Posh

TOWN CRIER SCROLL

Oyez! Oyez! Oyez! Hamlin town overrun by a plague of rats. Homes destroyed, children bitten, businesses ruined. Hold a meeting in the market place immediately to discuss and write down grievances. Two spokespeople will be appointed to read these out at the next town council meeting.

Each councillor writes a nasty letter to their Lesson 1 town partner. The townspeople are given a single piece of paper for an elected person to list the complaints about the plague of rats and their demands. Appoint the two spokespeople to read this out at the forthcoming meeting.

- COUNCILLORS DELIVER LETTERS

Townspeople spread out around the room as if they are at home. Councillors deliver the individual letters. Each town person in turn reads their letter out loud to the whole group.

- TOWNSPEOPLE RIP UP LETTERS

Councillors take up Lesson 1 council meeting still pose. Townspeople walk towards the councillors in slow motion with the letters they received. When all the townspeople are standing opposite their partners in the council chamber hold the letters above the councillor's heads and rip them up into small pieces, letting the pieces fall on top of them. The councillors must keep absolutely still. The townspeople stand back.

- THE MEETING

Everyone is present. The two appointed town spokespeople read out the list of complaints and demands. Appoint two new spokespeople to argue for the councillors and two for the townspeople. The four step forward but can only speak if holding one of the two sticks forcing them to take turns to argue their case with the councillors growing more arrogant and pompous and the townspeople ever more desperate. A child chosen to play the Pied Piper enters the meeting and promises to rid the town of rats ……. for a price.

LESSON 3

WARM-UP: Follow my leader.

- PIED PIPER SONG

Teach the children the song.

- PIED PIPER

Recreate the Lesson 2 council meeting with everyone present. Ask the Pied Piper (playing the recorder or humming) to enter the meeting playing the tune. He/she offers to rid Hamlin of rats. Spontaneously role-play everyone's reaction to this offer and a deal being struck.

- RATS

Ask everyone to be one of the rats living in Hamlin. The Pied Piper appears playing the tune and all the rats follow immediately and leave the town. Ask the students to role-play rats drowning in the river with a slow motion twisty/turning movement starting from a standing position and gradually spiralling down to lie perfectly still on the floor.

- BACK AT THE COUNCIL CHAMBER

Role-play the townspeople and councillors refusing to pay the Pied Piper for ridding the town of rats.

- CHILDREN OF HAMLIN

Ask everyone to be one of the children of Hamlin playing in the market square and choose a leader to immediately follow behind the Pied Piper. When the children hear the Pied Piper's tune they all join in singing and follow behind the leader in slow motion as if in a trance copying the movement of the person in front. A child chosen to play the lame child is left behind.

LESSON 4 GUIDED FANTASY

WARM-UP: Go over the song learnt in Lesson 3.

- PACK YOUR BAG

Explain that all the children of Hamlin are going on a journey. Ask everyone to find a space on their own and sit down, for a focused and calm beginning. Then ask them to imagine that they are packing a bag for the journey. The bag can only contain four items and all must be relevant to the journey. Shoulder tap volunteers to find out what is in the bag.

- CAVE DOOR

"You are going into a cave but there is no entrance. You will have to make your own."

Divide the class into groups of five or six and ask the students to devise a way that each group can become a door that the remaining students can open, pass through and close. Groups needs to work as a team to physically form the door without use of chairs or any other objects and can choose to have a password or bell ring for their door. All groups then pass through each door until everyone has passed through the final one and the students are all inside the cave.

• INSIDE THE CAVE

The children follow the narrative as you describe where they are and what they are doing.

"Inside the cave it is cold and dark. There is just enough light to see the way along a narrow path, icy water drips from the roof, mud squelches underfoot. You reach a narrow passage between rocks. Squeeze through in single file and edge along a narrow shelf along the rock edge, take care, there is a deep ravine to one side. Crouch down to move along a long dark tunnel. You suddenly find yourself in an enormous cavern with an underground lake. On the far side of the deep blue lake is a huge church carved out of the rock unlike any church you have seen before. There is a white sandy beach edging the lake and there are thousands of diamonds glittering like stars in the sand."

TASK
Stop to pick up diamonds and put them in your bag. You have been travelling for hours and feel hungry. The smell of delicious food fills the air. If you look across the lake you can just about make out a colourful spread of food at the top of a flight of steps leading up to the church. "How are you going to get across the lake to the food?" There are no boats.

TASK
Split into the cave door groups. This time each group is a boat that can carry one person across the lake. The boats move backwards and forwards ferrying passengers across. "When you arrive sit on the church steps."

TASK
Look at the amazing variety of foods and choose carefully before starting to eat. Think about what you are eating. "What it is?" "How does it taste?" Walk into the church and look around. Remember that it is unlike anything you have seen before. "What do the walls look like?" "What does the ceiling look like?" "Are there any paintings?" Describe the church. In a far corner discover a small door bearing an inscription: *'To open this door, first sing a song.'*

TASK
Sing the song you learnt in Lesson 3. The door opens, go through into a long corridor. Suddenly a strong wind starts to blow along the corridor and thousands of books fly past. Duck out of the way, crouch down and cover your head. The wind dies away and when you look up there are books strewn all over the corridor floor. Pick one up.

TASK
Each person in turn reveals the title of their book. Put the book in your bag. There is an empty room at the end of the corridor with four windows, one in each corner. Go in, discover that the windows are too high up to see out.

TASK

Ask for four volunteers to take a chair over to each corner of the room and look through the windows. "What does the place look like?" "What can you see on the horizon?" "What can you see nearby?" "Are there people or animals in sight?" "What can you hear and smell?" Choose a window to go through and bring back something from that other world in your hand. "What are you holding?" End by asking each child to decide between going to live in the world through the window or returning home to their family in Hamlin.

- *ADDITIONAL RESOURCES:* • *The Pied Piper* poem •   Robert Browning
Oxford Book of Narrative Verse
• *The Pied Piper* solo scene adaptation •
Heather Stephens, Cabbage
ISBN 0 9522224 5 0   Dramatic Lines

THE PIED PIPER'S SONG

Descant recorder

I'm a - ble by _ my se - cret charm to draw all crea- tures 'neath the sun that

sli - ther, fly - and run. Oh, come see that ma - gic place - so far from all harm.

music on the Greensleeves theme Veronica Bennetts

I'm able by my secret charm
to draw all creatures 'neath the sun
that slither, fly and run.
Oh, come see that magic place so far from all harm.

(Spoken softly by the Piper) Come, ... follow me.

Hilary Lewis

WALKABOUT

The students walk around the room at a steady pace without bumping into one another. Call out instructions at intervals.

"Walk ....

> fast
> drunkenly
> secretively
> looking up someone's nose
> looking down on somebody
> on ice
> on air
> through deep mud
> through a river
> through a minefield
> through a desert
> as if tired and sleepy
> as if angry
> as if sad
> as if happy
> as if shopping
> as if in a queue
> like a soldier
> like a tramp
> like a model
> like a ballet dancer
> like an old person"

And so on ....

- Movements and attitudes alter dramatically according to the instructions given.

ADDITIONAL RESOURCE: • attitude and change activities
Drama Lessons in Action • Antoinette Line
ISBN 0 9522224 2 6 Dramatic Lines

Rob Perrett

TABLEAUX

PREPARATION: Art books are often very expensive to buy so build up your own collection of suitable art postcards and prints and order books like *Paintings in the National Gallery* from the public library.

MAIN ACTIVITY: Take a picture, well known or otherwise, into class and ask the students to create it as a 'still'. Then suggest that they enact the five to ten minute lead up to that final pose ending with the still. Alternatively the students start with the still pose and enact the following five to ten minutes.

RESOURCE: • *Paintings in the National Gallery* •
Augusto Gentili, William Barcham & Linda Whiteley
ISBN 0 3168545 2 2 Little, Brown & Co

A selection of pictures suitable for this exercise from the resource book:

No. 44   page 55   *The Nativity*   Piero Della Francesca
No. 194   page 191   *Pharoah Pardons the Butler and Orders the Execution
                                 of the Baker**   Pontormo
              * Good to link with *Joseph and his Amazing Technicolour Dreamcoat*
No. 356   page 368   *Two Boys and a Girl Making Music*   Jan Molenaer
No. 471   page 467   *A Picnic*   Francisco de Goya
No. 559   page 554   *The Umbrellas*   Pierre Auguste Renoir

A general selection of paintings that are suitable for the exercise:

The Scream   Edvard Munch
Bathers at Asnières   George Seurat
The Dance   Antoine Watteau
Card Players   Paul Cézanne
La Primavera (The Spring)   Sandro Botticelli
The Blind Leading the Blind   Pieter Bruegel the Elder
Corn Harvest   Pieter Bruegel the Elder
The 28th July Liberty Leading the People   Eugène Dalacroix

- Some paintings will allow students to cover the lead up to the still pose, the still, and the follow on.

Mike Redwood

BRITISH BULLDOG

These exercises are based on the playground game British Bulldog.

BRITISH BULLDOG

One or two students stand in the centre of the room and attempt to either touch or stop the other members of the class as they try to move from one side to the other across the space.

SILENT BRITISH BULLDOG

Four or five students occupy the central space and are instructed to keep their eyes closed. The remainder of the students must get through without running and without being touched. There should be enough people in the centre of the room to virtually close off any obvious passageway through.

- These exercises are very demanding and require a great deal of concentration and stealth.

Stag Theodore

TRUE AND FALSE

Ask each student to think of a true story that has actually happened to him/her personally. It should be memorable and interesting.

> *i.e.* exciting, happy, sad, *etc.*

Next ask each student to concoct a false story that must be entirely fictitious but very plausible.

Each story is told to the whole group in turn with the students encouraged to guess which is true and which false. Discuss the differences. What made one story ring true? How can we use that feeling of 'actually being there'?

Next each student retells his/her story and mixes all the detail of the true story in with the false. What does the group think? How much of the story is believable? Does this story sounds more plausible than either of the other two?

Then discuss:
> expression
> feeling
> emotion
> the flow
> body language
> what the eyes are saying

Finally ask each student to reveal which story is true and which is false.

Leigh Conroy

21

PEKING JUMP!

This very simple exercise is suitable for all stages and requires no props or materials. It comes from the training practices of the Peking Opera Company and I learnt it taking part in workshops with them. It is good for focus, concentration and spontaneity.

The students kneel down facing the teacher and rest their body and weight right back on their heels. It is important that they are sitting right back and that their backs are straight. Complete silence is required.

Tell the students that you will clap your hands at some point and this will be the signal for them to jump to their feet in one fluid movement. The idea is for them to react to the signal without thinking and spring straight to their feet.

The students think that this is impossible because they are sitting back on their heels, and indeed if they think about it first it will be! They are amazed to discover that it is possible to spring up in a single movement and wonder how this was achieved!

It is a good idea to keep the students waiting focused for as long as possible and also to point out afterwards that in a dramatic sense that moment of anticipation is at the core of theatrical success; not necessarily what is happening but what may or is about to happen.

- This exercise helps with reactions and thoroughly focuses and concentrates the group as they do not know when the clap/signal will come.

Chris Durnall

I THOUGHT YOU WERE MY FRIEND

PREPARATION: Provide a folded note for each member of the class. On it is written:

I can't believe what you have done! I thought you were my friend!

MAIN ACTIVITY: Begin with each student sitting in a space on their own. Then give everyone the folded piece of paper with the written message. Explain that this note was discovered in their school bag after lunch before allowing the students to read it.

After each student has read the note ask them to imagine a situation behind the contents of the note. Hot-seat various students to find out what happened in their own particular story.

Next place the students in pairs and choose one of the scenarios to act out as a scene in which the two friends come face to face for the first time after the discovery of the note.

Then rehearse and perform.

Follow-on situations:

> The friends talk to parents.
> The friends talk to older or younger brothers/sisters.
> The friends talk to a teacher.
> The friends tell a wider circle of friends what happened.
> The day the friends make up.
> The day they first met.
> The day they became close friends.
> *etc.*

ADDITIONAL RESOURCE: • *The Best of Friends*
Pears Duologues • Heather Stephens
ISBN 0 9522224 6 9 Dramatic Lines

Lucy Heritage

THE MAGIC CORRIDOR

CROSSING SPACE/CREATING AN ENVIRONMENT

PREPARATION: First designate an area to represent a corridor down the centre of the room. This should be about ten feet/metres wide but can be wider if the room will allow. Ask the students to line up down one side of the corridor number off: 1, 2, 1, 2 and end up with Group 1 and Group 2.

MAIN ACTIVITY: You are ready to start the exercise. Ask the students to imagine that they are moving into a different world on stepping into the magic corridor. Each individual student must make every effort to shut out the rest of the class. Group 1 goes first and Group 2 leads on the way back.

Begin with a basic scenario.

> *e.g.* **Walking** ......
>
>> on stepping stones across a stream
>> through long grass
>> in the jungle
>> across the desert
>> through a crowded market

Next add another factor to a basic scenario.

> *e.g.* **Walking through long grass** ......
> *add* .... catching butterflies
>
> **Caught in a rainstorm** ......
> *add* .... a very strong wind
>
> **Walking down a pitch black corridor** ......
> *add* .... it is haunted
>
> **Walking briskly along a pavement** ......
> *add* .... a sheet of ice
>
> **Strolling along a beach** ......
> *add* .... a dog races up
>
> **Walking in the jungle** ......
> *add* ....a snake dangling from a branch

BUILDING A SCENE

This process can be used to build a whole scene by adding a new factor each time the students cross the space.

    e.g. **On a walk** ....
        add .... Victorian London
        add .... night
        add .... it is foggy
        add .... a dark alley
        add .... you are on your own
        add .... this is a dangerous part of London
        add .... you think you are being followed
        add .... you **KNOW** you are being followed
        add .... this is a dead end and you will have to go back!
        add .... you turn around and it is your best friend

N.B. This exercise can stimulate the imagination on many levels without getting into theory which may seem boring to many students as they automatically start to consider the '5 Ws':

- Where am I?
- When am I?
- Why?
- What am I doing?
- What for?

- Use the exercise in its simplest form for Stage 1 and as a scene building exercise for Stage 2 and Stage 3. It can also be used as a background exercise to create an environment prior to working on a script for the Stage 3 students.

Louise Winstone

TRAVELLING WARM-UP

The students sit in a semicircle. Then the first Caller announces by which means they must travel in order to change seats.

"Travel ......

> as an astronaut
> as a ballerina
> as a racing car driver
> as a WWF wrestler
> as an Olympic athlete
> as a soldier
> as if half asleep
> as if carrying something heavy or awkward
> as if sleep walking
> as if the floor is slippery
> backwards"

The Caller now decides who will be moving.

"Everyone .....

> here
> who lives in ...... (a place)
> who has been to ...... (a place)
> wearing something black
> with long hair
> with brown hair
> who has a cat
> who hates mushrooms
> with a birthday this month
> whose first name begins with ...... (alphabet letter)
> .... **move now."**

One person is always left standing because there is one less chair than number of students. That student then becomes the Caller and the procedure is repeated.

Ann-Marie Coulston

26

STAGECOACH DRAMA WORKSHOP

BACKGROUND: You have formed a new theatre company that has been commissioned to perform a work of improvised drama in the round lasting approximately ten minutes at a professional festival of the arts. Your aim is to produce and ultimately perform the work in front of an invited audience of influential adjudicators and theatre critics. If successful you will receive critical acclaim and possible stardom.

RESOURCES: • *sheets of A3 coloured card* • *marker pens* • (*STEP 9 POSTER*)

STEP 1
Decide who is going to be the overall director/producer of the theatre company. Who will make the decisions? Will the group have a say in the **initial** decision making or will this be down to the director? If you cannot agree take a vote.

STEP 2
Decide on a name for the theatre company.

- Remember it should be catchy or memorable.

STEP 3
Decide on the type of piece you are going to perform. Choose from the following:

> Murder Mystery
> Soap Opera
> Comedy
> Action/Adventure

STEP 4
Decide on the title of the piece. If you cannot agree wait until you have completed *STEP 7.*

STEP 5
Decide on the characters. Everyone must play a part with the possible exception of the director. Do not cast the piece yet.

STEP 6
Decide where the piece is to be set.

N.B.   You will not have a stage set. All props are to be mimed but use of available chairs is permitted.

STEP 7

Decide on the plot or what is going to happen in the piece and whether it is going to be one scene or a series of short scenes. You should have a **beginning** a **middle** and an **ending**. Also try to include something dramatic and/or a freeze frame, slow-motion sequence or flashback as these will increase the dynamics of the piece.

- Remember that there will be no lighting and only limited sound equipment will be available due to a generator failure at the arts festival! Please speak to one of the organisers if you require use of the sound equipment.

STEP 8

Hold auditions for each of the parts. The director has the final say - no arguments.

STEP 9

Begin rehearsals using the basic outline decided in *STEP 7*. Roughly block the moves, entrances, exits, etc. At the same time decide who is going to design a poster, handbill or programme entry to advertise the piece. Materials will be available from the festival organisers for this.

STEP 10

Continue rehearsals giving more attention to the dialogue

> *i.e.* What the characters need to say to move the story along.

- Remember that acting is living **truthfully** under an imaginary set of circumstances.

STEP 11

Repeat the scenes or sections that need work.

STEP 12

Rehearse again and again!

STEP 13

Give details of your piece to the adjudicators/festival organisers. Include your poster/handbill/programme entry.

N.B. The adjudicators will decide on a running order.

STEP 14

Performance!

STEP 15

Adjudication.

WORKSHOP NOTES

WARM-UP: We started with a dance and singing warm-up to maintain the three disciplines followed by drama warm-up games that required the students to form a circle in order to reinforce the 'in the round' performance aspect of the workshop. It was good to see how well the three stages interrelated; with Stage 3's guiding and helping Stage 2's and Stage 1's and, in some cases, vice versa! The school was split into four groups of ten at the end of the warm-up.

METHOD: Line up students in their stages with boys at the front. Then 'count' down the lines: 1,2,3,4, 1,2,3,4, until everyone has been allocated a number. Important, do not stop counting at the end of each stage but continue in the same sequence from the start of the next line. All 'ones' form a single group, all 'twos', all 'threes' and all 'fours'. You should end up with four groups and an even split of boys and girls from all stages. This method also helps to break up cliques of friends who always try to work together no matter how hard you try to split them up!

N.B. We spaced out the groups and sat students in a circle on chairs until *STEP 8* to keep them still and group focused with the less confident members remaining involved even if they were only listening.

MAIN ACTIVITY: We were then ready to distribute the first handout giving the background and setting out the Step 1 task. These handouts set out one step per page and we distributed them singly for the first couple of steps and then in batches of two, three or even four. We emphasised the importance of taking each step in turn and only moving on to the next after properly completing the previous one when a few students tried to jump ahead.

N.B.   The adjudicators/festival organisers referred to in the handouts are the three Stagecoach teachers who will adjudicate the festival entries and give 'awards' for best play, best performance, *etc.*

We gave assistance when required but the end product was entirely down to the groups themselves. The results were certainly entertaining and the plays ranged from "adequate" to "excellent" but they all contained at least one surprising performance, plot line or well-designed poster!

- This workshop was devised as a 'special' at the end of term for the whole school involving all three stages over three hours. However it could be also used for a one hour drama class or number of classes with adjustment.

Rick Ratcliffe

EFFECTS OF MOOD

HOT-SEAT WARM-UP: The students sit in a circle on chairs and express various moods through mime:

> feeling sad
> feeling happy
> feeling shocked
> feeling scared
> feeling angry
> being taken by surprise
> *etc.*

At any given moment everyone must freeze and selected students are asked to explain why they are feeling this way at this time. Stress that spontaneity is the key to the exercise.

TASK
In pairs, students act out a brief argument.

> *e.g.* Why didn't you turn up today?
> Why did you lie about all morning?

Rehearse and perform.

TASK
Larger groups improvise the following scenario:

> At 8 a.m. a mother rows with her daughter.
> She then rows with her husband before he leaves for work.
> The daughter is rude to her teacher at school.
> The father rows with his secretary.

The group discusses, rehearses and performs the linked situations with emphasis on the escalation of ill-feeling. Finally students should be encouraged to discuss how our changing moods affect others.

- Time scale 2-3 sessions to include discussion, hot-seating, rehearsal, performance, pair work and group improvisation.

Julie Nicholson

SORRY GAME

Two performers, one is static on a chair and must not speak but is able to react through body language to the mobile actor who is trying to apologise for doing something unforgivable:

killed the goldfish
stole a best friend
didn't show up
lost money belonging to the partner
lost the partner's mobile phone
forgot to deliver a message
spread gossip
copied him/her in an exam
put the partner's name down for the next Karaoke song
didn't invite the partner to a party
dropped a heavy weight on the partner's foot
etc.

The aim of the exercise is for the vocal actor to convince the other to accept his/her apology as quickly as possible and for the two to leave the stage area friends.

Lesley Ann Cole

INANIMATE OBJECTS

PREPARATION: Collect an assortment of inanimate objects:

> *e.g.*   a spoon
> a towel
> a bowl
> a football
> a jamjar
> a cushion
> a plate
> a banana
> a bed sheet
> a cereal box
> pair of shoes
> newspapers
> books
> empty tins
> *etc.*

Bring the assortment to the lesson. Sitting in a circle ask each student to improvise using an object as a prop but in a way **NOT** intended.

> *i.e.* a spoon is .... a microphone
> .... a dangling earring
> .... an ice lolly
> .... a canoe paddle

And so on .... but it cannot be a spoon!

Do this without allowing them time to think too long and hard about it. The spontaneity can be very amusing and will give you an insight into the way their minds connect.

If the exercise works well you can then place all the objects in the centre of the circle and invite students to perform random improvisations using the objects for purposes and in ways that were never intended.

Jane Bartlett

EXCLAMATIONS!

PREPARATION: Word process or write out a sufficient number of different lines that are appropriate to the scene for members of the class. Cut-up the lines individually, folding the paper so that they cannot be read, and put them in a large envelope.

> *e.g.* "He's got a gun!"
> "She's going to jump!"
> "They are going to steal something!"
> "He's terribly ill!"
> "She's in a foul mood!"
> "Help! The place is on fire!"
> "He quite clearly needs my help!"
> "Don't worry. It'll clean up!"
> "But you promised that you would!"
> "Look behind you!"
> "What are you going to do!?"
> "How could you do this to me!?"
> "Why did you do that!?"
> "I suppose you think that's funny!?"
> "How did you manage it!?"

In class ask each student to take a piece of paper but not to read it. Divide the students into groups of three and advise that one line is to be read at the beginning, one in the middle and one at the end of their scene.

Give the groups a scene idea to perform:

> A display being knocked over in a crowded supermarket.
> An incident at a wedding reception in an exclusive hotel.
> An accident that stops the show.
> Shooting on location.
> *etc.*

They then improvise the scene adding the unseen lines as directed and respond accordingly.

Lynette Gridley

33

TRAPPED

WARM-UP: Begin with a simple exercise, students working in pairs. All chairs should be placed at one end of the room in a line. A sits on a chair and B stands behind. A begins to make his/her way to the opposite side of the room. B must follow and stop A gently, by making contact. A is led back willingly and seated on the chair by B. A sets off again, B follows and stops A, returning him/her once more. Continue with A becoming more and more determined to reach the other side of the room and B equally determined to catch him/her. The pace of the exercise increases slowly until A is running and B is having to chase hard, stop A firmly and march him/her back to the chair. A's ultimate goal is to reach the opposite wall and B's is not to allow that to happen.

The students then change places.

N.B.   This exercise works well accompanied by rhythmic music.

MAIN ACTIVITY: Move on to an improvisation exercise, again in pairs. A is trying to book a hotel room for the night and B is the hotel receptionist. A can only communicate through 'closed' questions. No, Who? Where? What? Why? How? questions are allowed. B is not allowed to answer, no and must always reply,

> **"Yes, but ...."** and proceed to think up some excuse.

    e.g. **A:**   May I have a room for the night?

          B: **Yes, but ....** there's an elephant and two lions in there at the moment.

          A: Will they be gone by the time I need to go to sleep?

          B: **Yes, but ....** the rest of the circus may have joined them by then.

This is to encourage non-blocking improvisation.

Follow with another exercise designed to discourage blocking. In this improvised scene A and B are two prisoners sharing a jail cell. A begins with the initial idea of escape and a plan. B cannot dismiss A's ideas and must build on them and A cannot dismiss or belittle B's suggestions. Ultimately this is to encourage A and B to devise a complete escape plan between them however fantastic or ridiculous it might eventually prove to be!

Move to group work and divide students into small groups of four or five.
Ask each group to devise a still tableau with the title *Trapped*.

> *e.g.* **Trapped ......**
> > inside a trunk
> > in a lift
> > in a phone box
> > under an avalanche
> > in an exam room
> > a memory/thought inside someone's head
> > *etc.*

Ask each group to devise two more stills one to precede and one to follow on.

> *e.g. add ....* in a hurry
> **trapped in the lift**
> *add ....* emerging hours later
>
> *add ....* skiing off piste
> **trapped under the avalanche**
> *add ....* the moment of rescue
>
> *add ....* on the way to the exam
> **trapped in the exam**
> *add ....* getting the result
>
> *add ....* falling asleep
> **trapped inside someone's head**
> *add ....* waking with a start
> *etc.*

Ask each group to work out a scene for each tableaux with an introduction to the story, the moment of being trapped, and the resolution to the problem. Finally ask each group to perform a mini-play to the class making sure there is a definite beginning, middle and end. Ask for constructive criticism at the end of each presentation re clarity, favourite moments, performance qualities, *etc*.

Kate Lewis Smith

PHOTO STORIES

PREPARATION: Collect suitable photo strips from appropriate teenage magazines.

RESOURCES: • *sheets of white A3 card • black marker pens •*
(STORYBOARD & SPEECH BUBBLES)

Take photo relationship stories into class for the students to look at. Discuss the format and content of the various stories.

Then the students work in small groups of four or five on their own photo story ideas by scripting a storyboard.

Next they create still images of the photo story with one member of the group narrating the story and other members striking the poses. The students can make speech bubbles to raise above their heads.

Finally each group performs their finished story to the other groups.

N.B. An additional idea is to video the finished stories using the freeze-frame control on the video camera.

- Skills acquired:

    - all aspects of storyboard making
    - narration skills
    - mime and tableaux skills
    - group working skills
    - video and camera technique

Philip Jacobs

WELCOME TO THE STUDIO

Welcome to the Studio is a daily talk show which the teacher hosts and provides subjects for chosen guest/guests to talk about and discuss in front of a participating live audience. A student is picked from the class and asked to assume the character of a talk show guest and to improvise.

> *e.g.* You are a film star who has landed a controversial role.
> *add* ..... Your name has been linked to that of a famous pop star.
>
> You are a sports personality who has been accused of cheating.
> *add* ..... Publication of your book has caused an uproar.
>
> You won a fortune.
> *add* ..... And lost it overnight.
>
> The importance of your invention has been likened to the wheel.
> *add* ..... But your critics have hinted that you stole the idea.
>
> Your achievement has been likened to man's first moon walk.
> *add* ..... You shot to fame. How has this affected you?
> *etc.*

Every so often the host needs to prevent a guest becoming rooted by prompting, either firing a further question at the guest, passing the subject over to the other guests or handing it to the audience.

> *e.g.* "And that's when you became involved in the great disaster of ninety-seven, wasn't it? Tell us about that."
>
> "That's a very controversial statement. Let's see if anyone else agrees with you."
>
> "Hold on! I'd like to throw it open to the audience."
> *etc.*

- The host interviews each guest singly or seats four or five together and takes questions for the guest or guests from members of the audience.

Jeffrey Gilpin

FRIENDS AND ENEMIES

Two strangers meet and within one minute must become the closest of loving friends.

Alternatively two close friends meet and within one minute their mutual affection must turn to hatred.

- This challenging exercise is very enjoyable for performers and audience alike when successful.

Jenny Billington Earl

FROM BIRTH TO OLD AGE

Explain to the students that they are required to take time and use initiative with this exercise. The length of time will vary and is dependant on their ability. Music can be played to help them loose any inhibitions.

Begin by asking the students to curl up into the embryonic position on the floor or on a chair. Then ask them to uncurl very slowly and adopt the stance of a toddler. Follow this with the development from a toddler to a five or six year old, then the growth to an adolescent and follow through to an adult and finish with old age. Either talk the students through each stage or give a thorough explanation and allow them time to complete the exercise.

N.B. This exercise can be used to show students how to avoid stereotyping the ageing process. It also enables students to have the chance to work independently and to self-evaluate.

- Time scale ten to twenty minutes.

ADDITIONAL RESOURCES: • *The Old Person Remembers* •
• *The Young person Talks* •
from *Alone in My Room* monologues
Ken Pickering
ISBN 0 9537770 0 6   Dramatic Lines

Mandy Ribekow-Evans

POEM

Read through the poem.

The Children's fall-Out Shelter

Deep in their underground shelter
Three people sit in the dark,
Remembering how when they were children
The world was lit by a spark.

They were placed in underground shelters
By parents who did not survive.
They were packed into underground shelters
Like bees packed into a hive.

Tom had wanted to be a farmer
But the earth was bare as a stone

Bill had wanted to be a hermit
But found no place to be alone

Susan had wanted to travel
But the earth was covered in flame

So they sat in their underground shelter
Wondering who was to blame.

Now deep in their underground shelter
Three old people sit in the dark,
Recalling stories of the fire-flood
And of the fire-proof Ark.

Deep in their underground shelter,
Safe from poison and from flames,
They shape coffins out of the cradles
Upon which were written their names.

Brian Patten

'The Children's Fall-out Shelter' from GARGLING WITH JELLY
by Brian Patten
(Viking, 1985) Copyright © Brian Patten, 1995 reproduced with permission

MAIN ACTIVITY: Discuss the issues of environment in the future raised by the poem.

Pairs to work on relationships in the future relevant to the poem.

Work as a group on a relevant advertisement:

> *e.g.* a public awareness campaign
> a product that may protect
> a service
> an escape from the situation
> *etc.*

ADDITIONAL RESOURCE: Additional Brian Patten poems suitable
for use in this way include:
* *The Plague and the Fox* *
* *Tall Story* *
from a collection of poems *Gargling with Jelly*
ISBN 0 1403190 4 2   Puffin Poetry

Ben McAllister

DANCE
SECTION

HAPPY WARM-UP

Start in a circle holding hands.

This is based on the song, *If You're Happy*. Instead of the usual, 'If you're happy and you know it, nod your head' or 'stamp your feet' the dance teacher calls out instructions using the basic dance positions and steps.

> *e.g.* If you're happy and you know it, **point and close**.
> If you're happy and you know it, **point and close**.
> If you're happy and you know it,
> then you'll surely want to show it.
> If you're happy and you know it, **point and close**.
>
> If you're happy and you know it, **first and second**
> If you're happy and you know it, **second and third**.
> If you're happy and you know it,
> then you'll surely want to show it.
> If you're happy and you know it, **forth and fifth (***POSITIONS).***
>
> If you're happy and you know it, **plié now.**
> If you're happy and you know it, **plié now.**
> If you're happy and you know it,
> then you'll surely want to show it.
> If you're happy and you know it, **plié now.**
>
> If you're happy and you know it, **pirouette**.
> If you're happy and you know it, **pirouette**.
> If you're happy and you know it,
> then you'll surely want to show it.
> If you're happy and you know it, **pirouette**.

And so on ....

- The verses are easily tailored to suit each the needs of a class and the song provides an enjoyable way for students to learn basics and can be used again and again.

Ann-Marie Coulston

HAPPY WARM-UP

If you're ha-ppy and you know it, point and close. If you're
ha-ppy and you know it, point and close. If you're
ha-ppy and you know it, then you'll sure-ly want to show it, If you're
ha-ppy and you know it, point and close.

words adapted by Ann-Marie Coulston
original words and music Traditional American

DANCE EXERCISE IDEAS

- *LEGS*

Give the students loosening up exercises for the legs in class and suggest that they do them nightly in front of their favourite television programmes.

Saffron Smith

- *BODY*

Play some music to the students and encourage them to follow it through physicality by clapping, using head movements, punching forwards, upwards, etc.

Lucy Hamilton

- *HEAD*

Strong eye lines and head lines are important. Suggest that everyone wears a baseball cap and then challenge the students to flick it off onto the floor using the sharpest of head movements.

Samantha Jones

MOVEMENT IDEAS

MOVEMENT IDEAS EARLY STAGES STUDENTS

- DESCRIBING A CHARACTER

  Take music with a narrative like *Peter and the Wolf* and use
  descriptive movements to fit the music and each particular character.

  RESOURCES: • *Simply Prokofiev* •
  Decca
  • *Peter and the Wolf Narrated by Edna Everage* •
  Naxos

- MOVING IN AN ENVIRONMENT

  Cover different types of terrain:

  > walk in woods
  > walk through the jungle
  > walk along the beach
  > walk across the desert
  > walk in space
  > walk on hot coals
  > clamber over rocky ground
  > wade through water
  > crawl underneath something
  > leap over something
  > *etc.*

- GOING ON A JOURNEY

  Explore environments by taking the students on a journey and
  describing every detail.

- CIRCLES

  Explore the idea of circles and try to form a circle with every joint
  in the body.

MOVEMENT IDEAS STAGE 1 • 2 • 3 STUDENTS

- EXERCISES

  Floor exercises and using body weight to swing through to
  positions:

  - creating 'falls' and recovering
  - weight bearing in couples
  - spirals through the back
  - triplets
  - balance using the whole body

  Combine all these and teach to one another.

- DANCE

  Expand regular everyday movements into formalised dance shaping.
  Construct a dance through repetition, unison, stage direction and
  intention, *etc*.

Susie Reeves-Smith

FROGS

The students line up in one corner of the room and leap across on the diagonal, one at a time.

Tell the students they are frogs and that they need to cross the pond using lily pads. The pads are spaced quite wide apart so they must extend their feet each time in order to reach the lily pad. They must land safely or they will push the pad under the water and subsequently get wet. The back leg must also extend behind so it stays on the pad as long as possible.

Tell the students to try to leap on one level so as not to cause ripples on the surface which may distract the frogs behind.

Michelle Sills

FOLLOW MY LEADER

Two leaders are chosen from within the group and the remainder of the students line up behind them at one end of the room. The leaders start to move when the music begins and those standing behind have to copy their movements exactly.

TASK
The leaders travel through the available space:

> running
> skipping
> jumping
> rolling
> hopping
> on tiptoe
> walking in slow-motion
> balancing on a high wire
> *etc.*

Leaders should concentrate on high, middle and lower levels, using all the body parts.

> *i.e.* head, arms, legs, torso, *etc.*

- It is important for students to fully utilise the space provided and to vary the tempo of their movements.

Jane Price

TRAVELLING STEPS

The teacher chooses the Caller and asks him/her to suggest a travelling step for the class to perform around the stage or area designated as a stage. The Caller stands with his/her back to the class whilst this step is performed.

The teacher then asks the students to 'make a picture' inside any area of the stage and the Caller remains standing with his/her back to the class.

> *i.e.* downstage, upstage, stage right, stage left, *etc.*

Each student chooses a stage area and freezes in a still pose inside it on a given signal. The teacher then asks the Caller to shout out the name of an area.

N.B. The teacher asks the Caller to try again if there is no one there.

The Caller turns around and the student/students within that area scatter. Whoever is caught first by the Caller suggests the next travelling step.

And so on ....

Instead of making a picture introduce variations like limbering up or walking on the spot to the rhythm of crotchets, minims or quavers, *etc.*

- This game is very versatile and always popular with the Stage 1 students especially towards the end of a class.

Anneke Stephenson

CONTRASTS

WARM-UP: Introduce the idea of contrasts.

> *e.g.* soft tapping with toes
> stamping the whole foot on the floor
>
> reaching up to the ceiling
> stretching or bending down to the floor
> *etc.*

EXERCISE: Walking on the spot:

- 4 walks 'tall' stretching up to the ceiling
- 4 walks 'small' crouching down
- 4 walks legs astride and arms out to the side 'wide'

And so on ……….

N.B. After a couple of classes the students start contributing their own ideas.

> *e.g.* 'medium'
> 'three quarters'

Then progress to moving the exercise around the room, call out 4 walks in each position at random with the students also taking turns to nominate. A greater variety of movement begins to emerge when they move around the space.

> *e.g.* walking on hands and knees
> crawling
> slithering
> walking on stilts
> *etc.*

- The students enjoy this exercise and relish the opportunity to choose the movements and the challenge of finding new ones.

Angela Kelly

51

THE AUDITION

Explain how an audition works and then tell the students that they will be doing a shorter version in class to get into practice. Follow with a warm-up.

WARM-UP: Ten minutes.
An intense warm-up for Stage 2 • Stage 3 •

MAIN ACTIVITY: Begin the lesson by playing a piece of music for the students to listen to whilst catching their breath.

Next teach a 16 bar routine:

> *e.g.* Stage 1 • a show number to *Pick a Pocket or Two*
> Stage 2 • a show number to *Singin' in the Rain*
> Stage 3 • a 70's number to *Disco Inferno*

The students learn this piece for fifteen minutes only before they are split into groups of four or five, and then rotated. This gives them confidence to perform in front of each other.

The groups chose a winner themselves by a process of elimination. Then they all sit down and discuss the reasons why that student was judged the winner.

• The atmosphere is electric as I declare the start of an audition, the class concentrating fully, and the students can even be seen rehearsing when not dancing. We now do this on a regular basis and the students themselves choose the routine from the selection they have learned.

Sara McIntyre

THE STAGECOACH STRUT

Pupils choose the music which has to have a good, strong solid beat from a selection approved by the dance tutor.

Starting upstage from the diagonal, and one at a time, pupils improvise their own dance sequence with assistance from the teacher if necessary. Ideally the students keep to their own dance combination each time and build on the steps, develop more complex eye and hand co-ordination, and most importantly their own personal 'attitude' .... the more over the top the better!

PERFORMANCE: When the first dancer has completed the combination he/she moves to the back and starts a line, moving along slowly and rhythmically but with a care not to upstage the performer on the dance floor. When the final dancer has completed the combination and there is one straight line at the back, all the students leap forward performing cartwheels, handstands, whatever .....! and at a given signal with loud voices shout together,

"Yeah! Stagecoach Strut."

- Students are extremely enthusiastic and thoroughly enjoy all aspects of this work as it builds to the final performance. And audiences always respond with equal enthusiasm at demonstrations.

Joy Clarkson

ANGEL EYES

I like to make everyone feel comfortable when warming up and even the most 'left-footed' pupil feels at ease with this warm-up.

WARM-UP: Walk around the room in all directions to different rhythms, on different levels, styles building up to skips travelling both forward and backward, and then little runs in and out of one another.

DANCE ROUTINE: The Bruce Willis song *Angel Eyes* begins with the James Bond theme and has the sound of a door shutting and the bang of a gun, followed by the thud of something hitting the floor.

The students are secret agents and have to use their own imagination as they react to the sounds.

They might find themselves:

> chasing a villain
> being chased
> stalking a villain in undergrowth
> being stalked
> chasing through a car park
> being chased by villains in a car
> edging along a narrow parapet outside the 30th
> floor of a skyscraper
> diving for cover and dodging bullets
> *etc.*

RESOURCE: • *Angel Eyes* • from Dancing with a Stranger

• This idea lends itself to further individual or group development.

Jane Waring

GROUP CHOREOGRAPHY

The objectives of this exercise are to increase awareness of accuracy of movement, increase confidence, to blend as a group, and to achieve choreographic skills.

- Each student choreographs a short phrase, maybe 2 lots of 8.

- In groups of four each student teaches the rest of his/her group their phrase.

- Each group of four then links the four pieces of material together.

- Then each group teaches their routine to the rest of the class.

- Finally the teacher links all the choreography and the class work to perfect the new and now quite lengthy piece of work.

Pebs Jones

SINGING
SECTION

SONIC NAME DRAWING

This is a useful first day of term exercise when meeting and integrating new pupils into the group. It also provides important experience of listening to the spoken voice through musical ears and finding novel ways of notation whilst developing the skills of students who are already composing and performing their own songs.

RESOURCES: • wide selection of coloured poster paints • wax crayons •
• coloured marker pens • sheets of white A3 card/paper •

MAIN ACTIVITY: The students speak their names in a variety of different ways. Then choose the most 'beautiful' way to sing this and listen to the 'musicality' of the sound.

Points to listen for:

- rise and fall
- softness and richness of vowels
- spikiness
- scratchiness
- bounce of consonants

Ask the students which colours they associate with these sounds and if the colours are bright or pastel, warm or cold.

   e.g. scarlet or delicate pale pink
      navy blue or palest blue
      etc.

Ask them to describe the patterns they see.

   e.g. loopy
      spiky
      dotty
      soft curves
      etc.

Next students draw their names as they see/hear them. This Graphic Score can then be used as an additional resource in a variety of ways by the teacher.

Olivia Boot

TWO WARM-UPS

WARM-UP 1

Chewing gets the jaw and mouth muscles ready for singing.

Ask the students to pretend to chew toffees and to think of the flavour as they chew. Tell them to keep at it! Then ask them to chew gum and to blow huge bubbles. 'Pop' these at the appropriate moment!

WARM-UP 2

Use animal noises as a vocal warm-up.

Ask the students to make the sound of:

a snake .... sssssssss
a monkey ...... oo-oo, oo-oo
a cat .... me-ow
a dog .... woof
a sheep .... baa, baa
a duck .... quack, quack
a horse .... neigh
a lion .... roar, roar
a hyena .... ha! ha! ha!
a cuckoo .... cuckoo, cuckoo
a mouse .... eek, eek
a pig .... oink, oink
etc.

- The children find these warm-ups far more enjoyable than conventional exercises.

Lisa Broadhead

DON'T DO THAT GAME

This is an exercise that aids concentration and also helps with recognising rhythms.

PREPARATION: Decide on a specific rhythm to fit words or a phrase that students should **not** respond to:

> **"Don't do that."**
> **"Do not clap this."**
> *etc.*

MAIN ACTIVITY: The idea is for the teacher to clap a series of short rhythms and continue to keep them going with his/her foot and the class to clap the rhythms back keeping in time with the pulse. The exception is a **don't/do not rhythm** which must not be responded to by the students. Anyone who does is "out"!

The exercise can be made more difficult by playing the rhythms on a keyboard hidden in a medley so that they are less easy to recognise.

- I run the *Don't Do That Game* as a knock-out class competition and this make the exercise even more challenging with the complexity of the rhythms increasing until there is a final winner.

Marie Carter

MAMA DON'T 'LOW

Start by teaching *Mama Don't 'Low*.

Intro: Mama don't, no Mama don't, no Mama don't, no Mama don't, **NO!**

Verse 1:   Mama don't 'low no banjo playin' round here,
            Mama don't 'low no banjo playin' round here.
            I don't care what Mama don't 'low,
            gonna play my banjo anyhow.
            Mama don't 'low no banjo playin' round here.

Verse 2:   Mama don't 'low no guitar playin' round here,
            etc.

Verse 3:   Mama don't 'low no base playin' round here,
            etc.

Verse 4:   Mama don't 'low no talkin' round here,
            (gonna shoot my mouth off anyhow! ...)
            etc.

Verse 5:   Mama don't 'low no rock song singin' round here,
            (gonna sing my head off anyhow! ...)
            etc.

Verse 6:   Mama don't 'low no trumpet blowin' round here,
            etc.

Verse 7:   Mama don't 'low no bongo bangin' round here,
            etc.

Verse 8:   Mama don't 'low no tambourine shakin' round here,
            etc.

As soon as the students have learnt the song encourage them to substitute their own instruments. There are natural breaks in the music where they can imitate the instruments vocally as well as mime the action of playing them.

     e.g.   violin playing
            bagpipe blowing
            maracas shaking
            etc.

Then ask the students to suggest general ideas.

e.g. Mama don't 'low no acrobatics round here, ...

Mama don't 'low no skippin' round here, ...

Mama don't 'low no lazin' about round here, ...

Mama don't 'low no hoppin' round here, ...
etc.

Ask everyone in the class to suggest at least one thing that Mama don't 'low. Suggestions are often very funny and the students are kept interested, involved and focused for ages!

- This is a song that you can keep coming back to again and again because there are so many variations.

Sue Beard

MAMA DON'T 'LOW

Ma-ma don't 'low no ban-jo play-in' round here, Ma-ma don't 'low no

ban-jo play-in' round here, I don't care what Ma-ma don't 'low, gon-na

play my ban-jo a-ny-how, Ma-ma don't 'low no ban-jo play-in' round here.

Words and music Traditional

THE TELEPHONE SONG

The Telephone Song is a great way for students and teachers alike to learn names and is a gentle way of introducing solo singing. This activity works best if everyone sits in a semicircle.

Choose a student to go first.

CLASS: "Hi, Anna!"

ANNA: "I think I hear my name."

CLASS: "Hi, Anna!"

ANNA: "I think I hear it again."

CLASS: "You're wanted on the telephone!"

Anna picks another classmate.

ANNA: "If it isn't Lucy, I'm not at home!"

ALL: With a ric tic tickety tic, Oh yeah!
With a ric tic tickety tic, Oh yeah!

Then the song starts again with Lucy in the hot-seat.

CLASS: "Hi, Lucy!"

LUCY: "I think I hear my name."

And so on .... until everyone has had a turn.

- A Stage 1 student taught me this song! She had learnt it at school and it has proved to be an excellent icebreaker for Stage 1 and Stage 2 and even Stage 3 students on the first day of a new year.

Sue Beard

THE TELEPHONE SONG

Blues style, unaccompanied

"Hi, An-na!" "I think I hear my name." "Hi, An - na!" "I think I hear it a - gain." "You're wan - ted on the tel - e - phone!" "If it is - n't Lu - cy, I'm not at home!" With-a ric tic tick-e - ty tic, Oh yeah! With a ric tic tick-e - ty tic, Oh yeah!

"Hi, Anna!"
"I think I hear my name."
"Hi, Anna!"
"I think I hear it again."
"You're wanted on the telephone!"
"If it isn't Lucy, I'm not at home!"
    With a ric tic tickety tic, Oh yeah!
    With a ric tic tickety tic, Oh yeah!

"Hi, Lucy!"
"I think I hear my name."
"Hi, Lucy!"
"I think I hear it again."
"You're wanted on the telephone!"
"If it isn't John, I'm not at home!"
    With a ric tic tickety tic, Oh yeah!
    With a ric tic tickety tic, Oh yeah!

Words and music Traditional American

MY BONNIE LIES OVER THE OCEAN

This famous song is picked up almost instantly even by those unfamiliar with it and is an excellent warm-up used in this way.

WARM-UP: The exercise makes use of the number of **B** words in the song. The students begin sitting down, stand up on the first **B**, sit down on the second, stand on the third, *etc.* It is sung very slowly the first time round and progressively faster and faster using both verses or verse 1 only.

• When the students reach the chorus of the song it's absolute mayhem!

Steve Pritchett

MY BONNIE LIES OVER THE OCEAN

Verse 1:   My **B**onnie lies over the ocean,
              My **B**onnie lies over the sea,
              My **B**onnie lies over the ocean,
              0h, **B**ring **B**ack my **B**onnie to me.

Chorus.   **B**ring **B**ack, **B**ring **B**ack,
              0h, **B**ring **B**ack my **B**onnie to me, to me.
              Bring **B**ack, **B**ring **B**ack,
              0h, **B**ring **B**ack my **B**onnie to me.

Verse 2:   Oh, **B**low ye winds over the ocean,
              Oh, **B**low ye winds over the sea,
              Oh, **B**low ye winds over the ocean,
              And **B**ring **B**ack my **B**onnie to me.

Words and music Traditional Scottish

STAGE 1
STAGE 2
STAGE 3

NAME WARM-UP

WARM-UP: Stand the students in a circle and ask each to sing their own name aloud. Then go around the circle one by one and follow the scale from low to high and then back down again.

- When warming the vocal chords, singing teachers often use the scales with the 'ooh', 'aah' or 'lah' sounds. The *Name Warm-up* provides an interesting variation and can either be used instead of or in addition to these.

Ann-Marie Coulston

MOTIVATION

WARM-UP: Five to ten minutes, breath control and diaphragm strengthening exercises.

SID THE SNAKE EXERCISE

Breath control. Students fill their lungs and push the air out through their teeth in a controlled manner to see how long they can make the breath last.

LAUGHING POLICEMAN EXERCISE

Strengthening the diaphragm. Students put their hands on their stomachs and laugh 'ha, ha, ha', going up the scale, so they can really feel their diaphragms move.

MAIN ACTIVITY: Put simple movements to songs and encourage the students to use their own gestures in an effort to individualise the work. Students of all stages learn to be more confident and relaxed and the quality of their voices improves.

In addition to singing as a group break songs down into solo parts so that each voice can be heard. Choose two or three students to sing solo at the end of each lesson with the class commenting on the performances. This teaches the students to work well as a team, giving constructive praise and criticism to one another.

STAGE 2 • STAGE 3 • STUDENTS

Use pop song backing tracks, although these don't necessarily stretch the vocal ranges, it's a great way of teaching microphone technique. The students really enjoy singing their favourite songs and are then keen to attempt musical and classical numbers afterwards.

• Students can lack motivation in singing classes which might appear dull after 'exciting' dance and drama classes that keep them on the move. They need to be interested in learning to sing correctly so I have turned singing lessons into a form of performance training, teaching the solid foundations such as diaphragm and breath control, helping them to understand a song and relate to the words, and to learn to perform.

Joanna Legg

TRAFFIC LIGHTS

MUSIC GAME

To develop aural awareness, rhythm and pitch ....
......................and provide some light relief!

RESOURCES: • 1 red circular flash card • 1 green circular flash card •
(TO REPRESENT TRAFFIC LIGHTS)

Sing a song already learnt and use the flash cards to stop and start the
singing.

• The game ensures good, fun ensemble singing.

Carys Jones

MAJOR MINOR HAPPY SAD

MUSIC GAMES TO DEVELOP AURAL AWARENESS

The following games should be played for just a few minutes each week starting with Game 1 or possibly starting with Game 2 for Stage 3. As the students master a game move to the next level.

GAME 1

Play a major chord followed by a minor in root position or a minor chord followed by a major. Each student takes a separate turn and is asked to describe the chord formations as 'happy', 'sad' or vice versa. As the students become more proficient encourage them to use the correct terminology.

GAME 2

Play a single chord, either major or minor, in root position. Each student in turn is given his/her own major or a minor chord to identify. Make the game more difficult by using lower or higher chords on the piano to change the quality of the chord. Students that find this game easy can also be given inversions of chords and the addition of sevenths to identify.

GAME 3

This is the same as Game 2 but using major or minor arpeggios instead of chords. Also encourage each student to sing back the arpeggio when taking a turn.

GAME 4

Play a single note and ask each student in turn to sing a major or minor arpeggio in root position taking care not to use any notes that are too high! Assist as required making sure each student hears the 'correct' version played on the piano before moving on.

Tim Riley

SINGING TIPS

- ***VOICE STRAIN***

Stage 1 voices can get strained after a full lesson. One way to break up the hour is to use a story. Teach the students a short melody like *Three Singing Pigs, I know an old Lady* (who swallowed a fly) or *I Whistle a Happy Tune*. They sing this at various intervals throughout the lesson as the story is told. This gives them a short break as they listen to the story whilst keeping their voices warm at the same time.

RESOURCES: • *Three Singing Pigs* •
Making Music with Traditional Stories
K. Umansky ISBN 0 7136380 4 4
• *I Know an Old Lady* • • *I Whistle a Happy Tune* •
Apusskidu Songs for children

Beth Helsby

- ***HIGH NOTES***

If a student or a group of students are continually finding it difficult to reach a D note or higher have them raise the right arm quickly in conjunction with singing that note. The motion automatically raises the diaphragm helping the students to achieve the higher range.

Muriel Smith

- ***BREATH CONTROL***

To aid a student locate and control the diaphragm instruct him/her to blow up a balloon slowly. The diaphragm will automatically be used to perform this task and will need to be controlled as the student gradually blows up the balloon. This can also be used as a class competition in breath control both using the balloon and later the students' own voices.

C. Todd

• CONCENTRATION AND ARTICULATION

Popacatapetal.   The name of this Mexican mountain is perfect as a warm-up tongue-twister to improve concentration and articulation. Ask the students to sing it up and down a 5 note scale, one syllable for each note, singing the scale three times. The difficulty is that the stress comes on a different syllable every time but when this becomes too easy ask the students to sing the whole phrase on each note, gradually increasing the tempo at the same time.

Marie Carter

• BREATHY SINGING

To overcome the problem of "breathy" singing insert a thumb into the mouth and apply upward pressure against the roof, a tingling sensation is felt when the thumb is withdrawn. This area provides a focal point to direct sound and acts like a sounding board for the voice resulting in a clear ringing tone as the maxillary sinuses resonate and is particularly useful for production of a clear A vowel, 'ah'.

• CLEAR TONES

For the production of a clear ringing tone sing the consonant 'ng' with the teeth closed and the lips in a gentle smile exposing the teeth, enabling the maxillary sinuses to resonate. This helps particularly when an E vowel is sung immediately following an 'ng' sound, 'ng .... eeeeeeeeeee'.

• BREATHING

All singing requires the support of **rib reserve breathing** as it is technically called. An intake of breath using the diaphragm is followed by an inward and upward pull of the abdominal muscles. This supports a column of air under pressure beneath the larynx and keeps the chest expanded. Without this support the vocalist will be unable to sustain long phrases or project the voice adequately.

Catherine Lovett

RIFF GAME

The game develops improvisation and harmony singing, listening skills and rhythm. Use it alongside rounds and more conventional exercises. The class is divided into four or five groups.

GROUP 1:   Start the first off with a 2 bar riff which implies
                 simple harmony of the I-VI-IV-V or I-IV-V-1 type.
GROUP 2:   Is given a riff of their own to fit over the top.
GROUP 3 • 4: And the same for the other groups.

Parts are numbered from the bass upwards. Bring in each part individually and build up. Let the piece run so that all parts become secure. Confident groups can add and invent their own additional parts and students should be encouraged if they can 'hear' things that work.

- The pitch is suitable for Stage 2 • Stage 3 students. The base line may need to be revised for Stage 1 students.

Ian Wellens

AMERICA

This idea can be used as a warm-up exercise in its simplest form, as a singing workshop, or an individual item that can be expanded to take in the other two disciplines.

WARM-UP: Clap and stamp out the rhythm of the chorus of *America* from *West Side Story* as a rhythm exercise. The students usually realise that this rhythm is familiar to them.

MAIN ACTIVITY: Once the rhythm has been established give a brief outline of the plot of the musical and put the *America* number in context. Discuss song type and the style of singing required which is quite rough and brash, not angelic and soft. Spend time learning the melody line and the rhythms. Also spend time analysing the words and what they mean in context. Then it should be quite easy for the students to decide how each verse or line is to be performed.

Split the class into two, the girl's section to play the optimistic Puerto Ricans and the boy's section the more cynical group, and stage the song as a moving piece. The students should work in their respective groups but need to decide who should do what and which group should sing which line/verse, *etc*. Then discuss the whole song before putting it on the floor. The rhythmic clapping and stamping can be incorporated in the final version.

The finished piece needs to demonstrate how the song should be viewed as an integral part of a musical show. It also presents the opportunity for solo work, which most groups really enjoy, whilst allowing the tutor to assess each student in an informal way. And students are able to put their own personal stamp on a solo part and make an important contribution to the finished project.

N.B. No props are required for rehearsal but could be used if the piece is presented as a polished performance.

- The work can be covered in a one hour session or spread over several if the aim is a polished performance.

Janis Hopkins

CONTRIBUTORS

Claire-Louise Dunteavy, *Hartlepool.*
Jenny Billington, *Burton-upon-Trent.*
Trudy Hindmarsh, *Yarm.*
Bethan Morgan, *Penarth.*
Josephine Wells, *Wokingham.*
Natalie Jones, *Stevenage.*
John Almond, *Plymouth.*
Giuliano Neri, *Hartlepool.*
Hilary Lewis, *Norwich.*
Rob Perrett, *Swindon.*
Mike Redwood, *Kensington.*
Stag Theodore, *Plymouth.*
Leigh Conroy, *Colchester.*
Chris Durnall, *Penarth.*
Lucy Heritage, *Yarm.*
Louise Winstone, *Stevenage.*
Ann-Marie Coulston, *Kendal.*
Rick Ratcliffe, *Staines.*
Julie Nicholson, *Lancaster.*
Lesley Ann Cole, *Epsom.*
Jane Bartlett, *Barnstaple.*
Lynette Gridley, *Harlow.*
Kate Lewis Smith, *Southampton.*
Philip Jacobs, *Truro.*
Jeffrey Gilpin, *Mitcham.*
Jenny Billington Earl, *Derby.*
Mandy Ribekow-Evans, *Rickmansworth.*

Ben McAllister, *Cardiff.*
Saffron Smith, *Lancaster.*
Lucy Hamilton, *Epsom.*
Samantha Jones, *Hartlepool.*
Susie Reeves-Smith, *Plymouth.*
Michelle Sills, *Nottingham.*
Jane Price, *Penarth.*
Anneke Stephenson, *Beverley.*
Angela Kelly, *Truro.*
Sara McIntyre, *Preston.*
Joy Clarkson, *Truro.*
Jane Waring, *Harrogate.*
Pebs Jones, *Cardiff.*
Olivia Boot, *Harlow.*
Lisa Broadhead, *Rickmansworth.*
Marie Carter, *Roundhay.*
Sue Beard, *Melton Mowbray, Milton Keynes.*
Steve Pritchett, *Epsom.*
Joanna Legg, *Bournemouth.*
Carys Jones, *Swansea.*
Tim Riley, *Cardiff.*
Beth Helsby, *Lancaster.*
Muriel Smith, *Hartlepool.*
C. Todd, *Beverley.*
Catherine Lovett, *Northallerton.*
Ian Wellens, *Plymouth.*
Janis Hopkins, *Penarth.*

ADDITIONAL TITLES

All books may be ordered direct from:

DRAMATIC LINES   PO BOX 201   TWICKENHAM   TW2 5RQ
freephone: 0800 5429570   fax: 020 8296 9503

MONOLOGUES

THE SIEVE AND OTHER SCENES
Heather Stephens
ISBN 0 9522224 0 X

The Sieve contains unusual short original monologues valid for junior acting examinations. The material in The Sieve has proved popular with winning entries worldwide in drama festival competitions. Although these monologues were originally written for the 8-14 year age range they have been used by adult actors for audition and performance pieces. Each monologue is seen through the eyes of a young person with varied subject matter including tough social issues such as fear, 'Television Spinechiller', senile dementia, 'Seen Through a Glass Darkly' and withdrawal from the world in 'The Sieve'. Other pieces include: 'A Game of Chicken', 'The Present', 'Balloon Race' and a widely used new adaptation of Hans Christian Andersen's 'The Little Match Girl' in monologue form.

CABBAGE AND OTHER SCENES
Heather Stephens
ISBN 0 9522224 5 0

Following the success of The Sieve, Heather Stephens has written an additional book of monologues with thought provoking and layered subject matter valid for junior acting examinations. The Cabbage monologues were originally written for the 8-14 year age range but have been used by adult actors for audition and performance pieces. The Aberfan slag heap disaster issues are graphically confronted in 'Aberfan Prophecy' and 'The Surviving Twin' whilst humorous perceptions of life are observed by young people in 'The Tap Dancer' and 'Cabbage'. Other pieces include: 'The Dinner Party Guest', 'Nine Lives' and a new adaptation of Robert Browning's 'The Pied Piper' seen through the eyes of the crippled child.

ALONE IN MY ROOM ORIGINAL MONOLOGUES
Ken Pickering
ISBN 0 9537770 0 6

This collection of short original monologues includes extracts from the author's longer works in addition to the classics. Provocative issues such as poverty and land abuse are explored in 'One Child at a Time', 'The Young Person Talks' and 'Turtle Island' with adaptations from 'Jane Eyre', Gulliver's Travels' and 'Oliver Twist' and well loved authors including Dostoyevsky. These monologues have a wide variety of applications including syllabus recommendation for various acting examinations. Each monologue has a brief background description and acting notes.

DUOLOGUES

PEARS

Heather Stephens
ISBN 0 9522224 6 9

Heather Stephens has written layered, thought provoking and unusual short original duologues to provide new material for speech and drama festival candidates in the 8-14 year age range. The scenes have also been widely used for junior acting examinations and in a variety of school situations and theatrical applications. Challenging topics in Pears include the emotive issues of child migration, 'Blondie', 'The Outback Institution' and bullying 'Bullies', other scenes examine friendship, 'The Best of Friends', 'The Row' and envy, 'Never the Bridesmaid'. New duologue adaptations of part scenes from the classic play, 'Peace' by Aristophanes and 'Oliver Twist' by Charles Dickens are also included.

TOGETHER NOW ORIGINAL DUOLOGUES

Ken Pickering
ISBN 0 9537770 1 4

This collection of short duologues includes extracts from Ken Pickering's longer works together with new original pieces. The variety of experiences explored in the scenes are those which we can all easily identify with such as an awkward situation, 'You Tell Her', and the journey of self knowledge in 'Gilgamesh' whilst pieces such as 'Mobile phones', 'Sales' and 'Food' observe realistic situations in an interesting and perceptive way. Other duologues are based on well known stories including 'Snow White' and 'The Pilgrim's Progress'. Each piece has a brief background description and acting notes and the scenes have syllabus recommendation for a number of examination boards as well as a wide variety of theatrical and school applications.

MONOLOGUES AND DUOLOGUES

SHAKESPEARE THE REWRITES

Claire Jones
ISBN 0 9522224 8 5

A collection of short monologues and duologues for female players. The scenes are from rewrites of Shakespeare plays from 1670 to the present day written by authors seeking to embellish original texts for performances, to add prequels or sequels or to satisfy their own very personal ideas about production. This material is fresh and unusual and will provide exciting new audition and examination material. Comparisons with the original Shakespeare text are fascinating and this book will provide a useful contribution to Theatre Study work from GCSE to beyond 'A' level. Contributors include James Thurber (Macbeth) Arnold Wesker (Merchant of Venice) and Peter Ustinov (Romanoff and Juliet). The collection also includes a most unusual Japanese version of Hamlet.

SCENES

JELLY BEANS

Joseph McNair Stover
ISBN 0 9522224 7 7

The distinctive style and deceptively simple logic of American writer Joseph McNair Stover has universal appeal with scenes that vary in tone from whimsical to serious and focus on young peoples relationships in the contemporary world. The collection of 10-15 minute original scenes for 2, 3 and 4 players is suitable for 11 year olds through to adult. Minimal use of sets and props makes pieces ideal for group acting examinations, classroom drama, assemblies and various other theatrical applications and have been used with success at Young Writers Workshops to teach the elements of script writing and dramatic development.

ONE ACT PLAYS

WILL SHAKESPEARE SAVE US!
WILL SHAKESPEARE SAVE THE KING!

Paul Nimmo
ISBN 0 9522224 1 8

Two versatile plays in which famous speeches and scenes from Shakespeare are acted out as part of a comic story about a bored king and his troupe of players. These plays are suitable for the 11-18 year age range and have been produced with varying ages within the same cast and also performed by adults to a young audience. The plays can be produced as a double bill, alternatively each will stand on its own, performed by a minimum cast of 10 without a set, few props and modern dress or large cast, traditional set and costumes. The scripts are ideal for reading aloud by classes or groups and provide an excellent introduction to the works of Shakespeare. Both plays have been successfully performed on tour and at the Shakespeare's Globe in London.

SUGAR ON SUNDAYS AND OTHER PLAYS

Andrew Gordon
ISBN 0 9522224 3 4

A collection of six one act plays bringing history alive through drama. History is viewed through the eyes of ordinary people and each play is packed with details about everyday life, important events and developments of the period. The plays can be used as classroom drama, for school performances and group acting examinations and can also be used as shared texts for the literacy hour. The plays are suitable for children from Key Stage 2 upwards and are 40-50 minutes in length and explore Ancient Egypt, Ancient Greece, Anglo-Saxon and Viking Times, Victorian Britain and the Second World War. A glossary of key words helps to develop children's historical understanding of National Curriculum History Topics and the plays provide opportunities for children to enjoy role play and performance.

TEENAGE PLAYS

X-STACY	Margery Forde
	ISBN 0 9522224 9 3

Margery Forde's powerful play centres on the rave culture and illicit teenage drug use and asks tough questions about family, friends and mutual responsibilities. The play has proved hugely successful in Australia and this English edition is published with extensive teachers' notes by Helen Radian, Lecturer of Drama at Queensland University of Technology, to enrich its value for the secondary school classroom, PSHE studies, English and drama departments.

WHAT IS THE MATTER WITH MARY JANE?	Wendy Harmer
	ISBN 0 9522224 4 2

This monodrama about a recovering anorexic and bulimic takes the audience into the painful reality of a young woman afflicted by eating disorders. The play is based on the personal experience of actress Sancia Robinson and has proved hugely popular in Australia. It is written with warmth and extraordinary honesty and the language, humour and style appeal to current youth culture. A study guide for teachers and students by Dianne Mackenzie, Curriculum Officer for English and Drama, New South Wales is included in this English edition ensuring that the material is ideal for use in the secondary school classroom and for PSHE studies, drama departments in schools and colleges in addition to amateur and professional performance.

RESOURCES

DRAMA LESSONS IN ACTION	Antoinette Line
	ISBN 0 9522224 2 6

Resource material suitable for classroom and assembly use for teachers of junior and secondary age pupils. Lessons are taught through improvisation. These are not presented as 'model lessons' but provide ideas for adaptation and further development. The lessons include warm-up and speech exercises and many themes are developed through feelings such as timidity, resentfulness, sensitivity and suspicion. The material can be used by groups of varying sizes and pupils are asked to respond to interesting texts from a diverse selection of well known authors including: Roald Dahl, Ogden Nash, Ted Hughes, Michael Rosen, Oscar Wilde and John Betjeman.

RESORCES

AAARGH TO ZIZZ 135 DRAMA GAMES

Graeme Talboys
ISBN 0 9537770 5 7

This valuable resource material has been created by a drama teacher and used mostly in formal drama lessons but also in informal situations such as clubs and parties. The games are extremely flexible, from warm up to cool down, inspiration to conclusion and from deadly serious to purest fun and the wide variety ranges from laughing and rhythm activities to building a sentence and word association. Games such as Do You Like Your Neighbour? could be used as part of a PSHE programme together with many of the activities connected with 'fair play'. The games are easily adapted and each has notes on setting up details of straightforward resources needed. All this material has been used with a wide range of young people in the 10 - 18 year age range.

MUSICAL PLAYS

THREE CHEERS FOR MRS BUTLER

adapted by Vicky Ireland
ISBN 0 9537770 4 9

This versatile musical play about everyday school life is for anyone who has ever been to school. It features the poems and characters created by Allan Ahlberg with songs by Colin Matthews and Steven Markwick and was first performed at the Polka Theatre for Children, London. The two acts of 40 minutes each can be performed by children, adults or a mixture of both and the play can be produced with a minimum cast of 7 or a large cast of any size.

INTRODUCING OSCAR
The Selfish Giant & The Happy Prince

Veronica Bennetts
ISBN 0 9537770 3 0

Oscar Wilde's timeless stories for children have been chosen for adaptation because of the rich opportunities offered for imaginative exploration and the capacity to vividly illuminate many aspects of the human condition. The original dialogue, lyrics and music by Veronica Bennetts can be adapted and modified according to the needs of the pupils and individual schools or drama groups. The Selfish Giant runs for 25 minutes and The Happy Prince for 1 hour 15 minutes. Both musical can be used for Trinity College, *London.* examinations and are ideal for end of term productions, for drama groups and primary and secondary schools.